THE BLACKTIP REEF SHARK

By Sara Green

BELLWETHER MEDIA • MINNEAPOLIS, MN

Jump into the cockpit and take flight with Pilot books. Your journey will take you on high-energy adventures as you learn about all that is wild, weird, fascinating, and fun!

This edition first published in 2013 by Bellwether Media, Inc.

No part of this publication may be reproduced in whole or in part without written permission of the publisher. For information regarding permission, write to Bellwether Media, Inc., Attention: Permissions Department, 5357 Penn Avenue South, Minneapolis, MN 55419.

Library of Congress Cataloging-in-Publication Data

Green, Sara, 1964-
 The blacktip reef shark / by Sara Green.
   pages cm. – (Pilot. Shark fact files)
 Summary: "Engaging images accompany information about the blacktip reef shark. The combination of high-interest subject matter and narrative text is intended for students in grades 3 through 7" –Provided by publisher.
 Includes bibliographical references and index.
 ISBN 978-1-60014-867-5 (hardcover : alk. paper)
 1. Blacktip shark–Juvenile literature. I. Title.
 QL638.95.C3G737 2013
 597.3'4–dc23
                              2012029806

TABLE OF CONTENTS

BLACKTIP REEF SHARK
IDENTIFIED

Schools of colorful fish dart around a **coral reef** in the Pacific Ocean. Suddenly, a brownish gray shark approaches the reef. It is hunting for a meal. The shark's fins look like they've been dipped in black paint. This is the blacktip reef shark. The fish scatter, but the shark is a fast predator. It pursues them and catches several fish in one bite. After satisfying its hunger, the shark swims peacefully among the reef fish in the cool, blue water.

Blacktip reef sharks live in the Pacific Ocean, the Indian Ocean, and the Mediterranean Sea. They prefer to swim in shallow waters around coral reefs, lagoons, and mangrove forests. They occasionally enter bodies of freshwater.

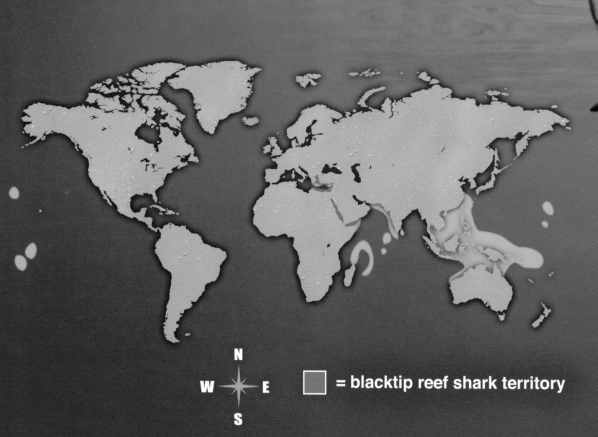

N
W—E
S

= blacktip reef shark territory

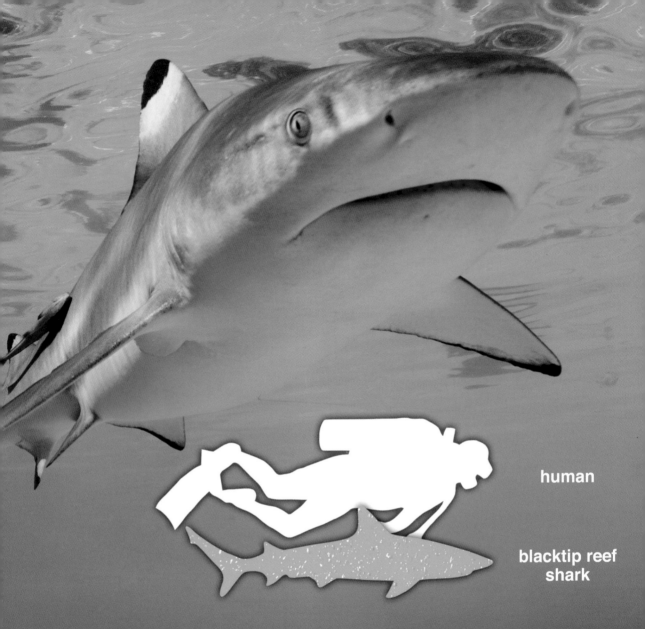

human

blacktip reef shark

The average blacktip reef shark measures 6 feet (1.8 meters) long and weighs up to 100 pounds (45 kilograms). The shark's coloring is an example of **countershading**. Its dark back and pale belly blend in with the ocean's colors. This helps the shark sneak up on prey and hide from predators.

A streamlined body and rounded snout help the blacktip reef shark swim through water with ease. Its skin is covered with a layer of **dermal denticles**. These overlapping scales help the shark move quickly and quietly through the water. The shark's skeleton is made of **cartilage**. This lightweight tissue is more flexible than bone. It allows the shark to bend and make quick turns when it chases prey.

The blacktip reef shark has two **dorsal fins**, one large and one small. These keep the shark upright and balanced. The larger fin displays a brilliant white band beneath its black tip. Two **pectoral fins** help the shark steer. The shark gains speed by moving its strong tail fin from side to side.

TIP-OFF

The blacktip reef shark's large dorsal fin often sticks out of the water as it swims in shallow areas.

NO TWO ARE ALIKE

Researchers can recognize individual blacktip reef sharks by the markings on their dorsal fins. The border pattern between the black and white colors is different for each shark.

dorsal fin —

pectoral fins

BLACKTIP REEF SHARK
TRACKED

Female blacktip reef sharks are **viviparous**. Eggs hatch in the mother, and the babies grow inside of her. When the babies are fully developed, the mother swims to a shallow, sandy area near shore. She gives birth to a litter of 2 to 4 live young called pups. Each pup is 13 to 20 inches (33 to 51 centimeters) long and has a full set of teeth. The mother swims away after giving birth. The pups remain in shallow waters until they are large enough to defend themselves against predators.

Sharks **mature** slower than other types of fish. Blacktip reef sharks become adults when they are 8 or 9 years old and 3 feet (1 meter) in length. They live around 12 years.

Blacktip reef sharks sometimes leap out of the water when chasing fish. This move is called a breach. Only a few other types of sharks can do this.

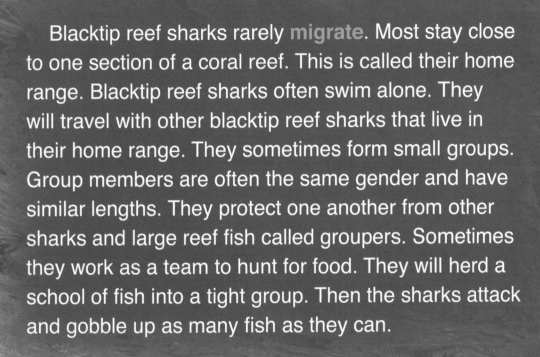

Blacktip reef sharks rarely **migrate**. Most stay close to one section of a coral reef. This is called their home range. Blacktip reef sharks often swim alone. They will travel with other blacktip reef sharks that live in their home range. They sometimes form small groups. Group members are often the same gender and have similar lengths. They protect one another from other sharks and large reef fish called groupers. Sometimes they work as a team to hunt for food. They will herd a school of fish into a tight group. Then the sharks attack and gobble up as many fish as they can.

Blacktip reef sharks use their keen senses to find food in coral reefs. Even when the light is dim, they can spot prey with their large, round eyes. Water flows through their nostrils to allow them to smell prey. The **ampullae of Lorenzini** are small pores in their snouts. These sense the weak **electric fields** of animals that live in the water. The sharks also have sensors called **lateral lines** that run the length of their bodies. Lateral lines help sharks sense the movement of prey in the water. These highly developed senses allow blacktip reef sharks to quickly locate their prey.

KEEP SWIMMING

Oxygen-rich water flows over a shark's gills as it swims. The blacktip reef shark must swim constantly in order to breathe.

Blacktip reef sharks feast on smaller fish, such as mullet and wrasse. They also eat squids, octopuses, shrimp, and sea snakes. Their long, **serrated** teeth are well suited for a diet of reef fish. They grow in several rows. When front teeth break or fall out, new teeth from back rows move up to take their place.

GUARDIAN SHARKS

In Hawaii, some families consider blacktip reef sharks to be *aumakua*, or guardian spirits that offer help when needed.

Blacktip reef sharks are not aggressive toward people. Most will swim away from humans who enter their territory. Some are curious and will investigate. These sharks are usually harmless. However, a few have been known to bite swimmers or people wading in shallow water.

BLACKTIP REEF SHARK

CURRENT STATUS

The global population of blacktip reef sharks is not currently in danger. However, many scientists worry about the shark's future. Blacktip reef sharks swim in shallow waters and are easy targets for fishers. Many end up as **bycatch** in nets meant for other fish. People eat their meat and use their fins to make shark fin soup. Their livers are valued for their oil. Each year, more blacktip reef sharks are caught than are born. The International Union for Conservation of Nature (IUCN) has given the blacktip reef shark a near threatened rating.

SHARK BRIEF

Common Name: **Blacktip Reef Shark**

Also Known As: **Black Fin Reef Shark**
Black Tips Nilow
Guliman

Claim to Fame: **Black fin tips that stick up above the water's surface**

Hot Spots: **Hawaii**
Northern Australia
South Pacific Islands

Life Span: **12 years**

Current Status: **Near Threatened (IUCN)**

EXTINCT

EXTINCT IN THE WILD

CRITICALLY ENDANGERED

ENDANGERED

VULNERABLE

NEAR THREATENED

LEAST CONCERN

Many of the ocean's coral reefs are in danger because of pollution and warmer water temperatures. Without a healthy home range, blacktip reef sharks cannot thrive. Fortunately, people around the world are working to save the coral reefs. They teach others to treat coral reefs and the animals that live in them with care.

The blacktip reef shark is one of the few types of sharks that do well in aquariums. People can view these sharks up close without traveling to the ocean. A great place to observe blacktip reef sharks is the Shedd Aquarium in Chicago, Illinois. Blacktip reef sharks swim among rainbow-colored fish in the coral gardens of the Wild Reef exhibit. When the sharks approach the glass wall, visitors feel their hearts pound with excitement!

GLOSSARY

ampullae of Lorenzini—a network of tiny jelly-filled sacs around a shark's snout; the jelly is sensitive to the electric fields of nearby prey.

bycatch—animals that are accidentally caught with fishing nets or lines

cartilage—flexible connective tissue that makes up a shark's skeleton

coral reef—a structure made of coral that usually grows in shallow seawater

countershading—coloring that helps camouflage an animal; fish with countershading have pale bellies and dark backs.

dermal denticles—small tooth-like scales that cover some types of fish

dorsal fins—the fins on the back of a fish

electric fields—waves of electricity created by movement; every living being has an electric field.

freshwater—water that has little to no salt; lakes, ponds, rivers, and streams contain freshwater.

lagoons—shallow bodies of water separated from the sea by sand or reefs

lateral lines—a system of tubes beneath a shark's skin that helps it detect changes in water pressure

mangrove forests—swampy areas of trees and shrubs along coastlines

mature—to become old enough to reproduce

migrate—to travel from one place to another, often with the seasons

near threatened—could soon be at risk of becoming endangered

pectoral fins—a pair of fins that extend from each side of a fish's body

serrated—having a jagged edge

viviparous—producing young that develop inside the body; viviparous animals give birth to live young.

TO LEARN MORE

At the Library

Ellwood, Nancy. *Sharkpedia*. New York, N.Y.: DK Publishing, 2008.

Musgrave, Ruth. *National Geographic Kids Everything Sharks*. Washington, D.C.: National Geographic, 2011.

Star, Fleur. *Shark*. New York, N.Y.: DK Pub., 2009.

On the Web

Learning more about blacktip reef sharks is as easy as 1, 2, 3.

1. Go to www.factsurfer.com.

2. Enter "blacktip reef sharks" into the search box.

3. Click the "Surf" button and you will see a list of related Web sites.

With factsurfer.com, finding more information is just a click away.

INDEX